GW00738379

To STEPHEN

lots of love

Suki Thompson
Co-founder & Chair Oystercatchers,
Executive Director Xeim

Creativity is back.
And I couldn't be more excited.

As marketers, we've all watched tech and data dominate discussion, for all the right reasons, bringing us personalised marketing and opening doors to all sorts of exhilarating brand experiences. In contrast, creativity's role, as a driver of growth, slipped down the business agenda.

Happily, the scales have re-balanced. Last year, Britain's creative industries smashed through the £100 billion barrier and brands began their journey to put creative back into the heart of business.

I believe that creativity helps us innovate, make connections we hadn't seen before, break open problems, and create not just works of art but 'arts of work'. Work-related products and ideas that don't just solve strategic problems, but also surprise, delight and change behaviour. David Attenborough's Blue Planet II's newborn whale imagery is probably the best ad of our time.

In this fabulous book, Creative Influence, we showcase, through portraits by iconic photographer and agency leader, Rankin, some of the most influential creative leaders in marketing today. Every single person we feature is recognised as a star, for producing creative alchemy that builds business and brands. They nurture, persuade, and break the rules to trailblaze creativity with purpose.

Creative Influence inspires us all with comments on what creativity looks like to this remarkable line-up of groundbreakers, and, with Rankin's beautiful photography, shares a glimpse into each of their creative souls. Thank you to The Fifth, the influencer agency, who has partnered us in the development of this book and to everyone who generously gave their time to make this project possible.

Sit back, relax, enjoy reading this book, and let your creativity flourish.

Rankin
Photographer, Publisher and
Founder of THE RANKIN GROUP

Creativity is at its best when we gain inspiration from each other. With my long history in publishing and magazines, this is something that I truly value and have seen lead to some amazing and unexpected results.

People's opinions and ideas only make yours better; you can't be precious; you can't be a clichéd 'lone wolf'. You have to work with people, be humble and understand that there's always someone out there with something more interesting to say or add than you. Without a shadow of a doubt, this lesson has elevated each and every piece of work that I have been a part of and has helped me to be a better artist, curator and creative person in general.

That's why I have designed RANKIN to be a haven of creative collaboration; under one roof we have the entire production process from start to finish, allowing everyone to give their unique opinion and have their say.

This attitude and ability to listen is so important to moving forward both creatively and culturally. The social divisiveness that we are seeing in the world right now can only be confronted by an ability to gain understanding from the people around us – not forgetting the ones outside our own mini echo chambers.

To me, that's what creativity is about, getting individuals to see things from a different perspective, while expanding your own unique outlook.

Hopefully, we can all do this together to help make the world a better place!

RANKIN

Oliver Lewis,
Founder & Managing Director,
THE FIFTH

We are witnessing a social revolution in creativity and as a result the face of influence is changing before our eyes.

We are entering a new age of the entrepreneur, where creativity and storytelling have been democratised. Where life can be your canvas and where relatability and authenticity are now a commodity.

A recent study found that 31% of children between the ages of 11–16 aspired to be a social media influencer or YouTube creator, second and third only to becoming a doctor. It's safe to say, Gen Z is shaping up to be one of the most entrepreneurial generations in history. The internet has not only enabled them to build communities and be creative with them in ways that we couldn't have imagined, it has given birth to a new world order of creators and storytellers, who have realised the merits of inclusivity.

To some this may be unwanted, possibly even unwarranted, but disruption only ever helps to raise the bar and serves as a necessary warning against complacency and the mediocrity of the status quo. So we are only ever faced with one choice if we strive to move forward; to adapt to the new world, to embrace change and encourage more to do the same.

There is no finer example of a creative icon, entrepreneur and pacesetter who continues to embrace this revolution than Rankin; one who understands that wider collaboration is a keystone to the future. And Oystercatchers, which creates extraordinary business partnerships and has bought together these marketing influencers that make a difference to our brands every day.

Here at The Fifth we are delighted to partner Oystercatchers and Rankin in this book. I am honoured in this small way to be part of their vision and true celebration of talent, inclusivity and creativity.

I hope that we inspire more to follow suit and champion creative diversity and positive change.

Creativity. More important than ever before in marketing. A product of discipline, rigour, great use of data and imagination.

To connect, inspire and move, great art, architecture and advertising all need to put the heart before the head.

As Maya Angelou so beautifully said, 'People will forget what you said, people will forget what you did, but people will never forget how you made them feel'.

David Wheldon
CMO
RBS

Deborah Dolce
SVP, Group Brand & Marketing Director
TJX Europe

Creativity, a word that is bandied around a great deal. In its broadest sense, it might be used to critique work, to shine a light on someone's thought process or to illustrate an unusual solution to a problem.

At the heart of all of these is the idea of making or doing something out of the ordinary, beyond expectations, something just more brilliant than the known. And its whole purpose is to communicate an idea or thought, a meaning to its audience whether it's marketing, art or even a movement.

Creativity seems to be born from a cocktail of knowledge and understanding mixed with originality and flair. But I think the greatest enabler to creativity must be courage.

If we can remove shackles and boundaries, if we can be bold, if we can let imaginations run free, then we really might get to make, or at the very least see, something truly amazing.

Creativity is asking 'what if?' and having the desire, confidence and drive to turn that question into a conversation, a concept and ultimately, an output. The word 'output' is purposefully vague/broad, as the creative approach and mindset can be applied to everything from the creation of a piece of art, to the development of an ad campaign, or a new iteration of a process.

As marketing leaders, I believe it's our responsibility to create environments that support and stimulate creativity. To nurture the curious 'what if?' spirit, three core values must be in place:

Positive challenge. It can't just be ok to challenge the status quo, it should be expected. Hierarchy needs to be irrelevant.

Embracing failure. You can remove the fear of trying by recognising the value of a failed attempt. The insight failure generates is of huge value in understanding how to improve and build a better next iteration. Setting up a 'fail fast and cheap' testing framework is important.

Customer. Creativity needs to start with a clear objective rooted in customer understanding. Using data and quality insight to drill down into a need or issue, is key to ensuring the right question is being answered.

Ed Madden
Head of Marketing
nPower

Creative is an adjective not a noun. That means it isn't a job on its own, it's a measure of how you do whatever job you do: Creative Marketer, Creative Strategist, Creative Executive. In communications, creative is what separates the extraordinary from the ordinary and that will be different every time – there can't be a formula for that. But a good guide is, if the work doesn't make us feel slightly nervous, then we haven't pushed ourselves far enough.

Sharry Cramond
Marketing Director, Food & Hospitality
Marks & Spencer

Keith Moor
CMO
Santander

Creativity to me is about an individual's freedom of expression. It's about the ability to find ways to do things that can deliver solutions to problems, create ideas that inspire and never being afraid to explore.

I don't think it's about being necessarily different and radical. Of course, this can be the case, however, there are plenty of examples of creativity borne of structure, form and rigidity. It is much more about a state of mind, an exploratory mindset if you will, a desire to learn and grow and ultimately to not be afraid to try new things in the search for what one is looking for.

I see this every day in my children and wonder when I lost their inherent sense of creativity. I often wonder what I could have done to never lose it in the first place. But instead of spending wasted time thinking about this question, I instead look at the creativity of my children as my inspiration. I strive to see the world through their eyes when I need to unlock my own creativity and always break complex problems down to their simplest form. I find that this is at the heart of allowing creativity to thrive.

Despite the radical changes happening around us, creativity in marketing, at its heart, is still about truly understanding the customer and the role the brand plays in their lives. Relevant application of data can deepen this understanding, unlocking insight on the entire customer experience and thereby driving loyalty and advocacy further.

Emily Somers
CMO
Domino's

Marketers hold one secret weapon that the rest of the business doesn't. Creativity.

A simple, yet powerful idea that can make the hairs on the back of your neck stand up. But in today's world, getting to great creative is not always easy, but more important than ever. People are bombarded with on average 10,000 brand messages a day. Which is why we need to be brave, take risks and create work that might get criticised but breaks through the clutter and fuels conversation.

Talkability and fame drive 4x higher brand communication effectiveness and 50–80% of return on investment is driven by the creative work. Great creative ideas influence culture, become popular, are loved and ultimately grow business. As the world we market in changes, it's critical we focus on the power of great creative.

Keith Weed
Former Chief Marketing
& Communications Officer
Unilever

Kerris Bright
Chief Customer Officer
BBC

Creativity is the uniquely and deeply human ability to go beyond the obvious.

Creativity is allowing yourself to think outside the box. To colour outside the lines. To take risks, be brave, and innovate. It's that sharp intake of breath, the 'double take' to let it sink in. To take people by surprise, to trigger you to look at something in a different light, and to engage a new audience that (perhaps) never before engaged.

Creativity makes you feel something you've never felt before, to connect you with a new brand or movement that you may not have known, or appreciated, previously.

It harnesses insights into human emotion to deliver a personal experience. It uses technology to engage people in new ways. It's the ripple of conversations after seeing something amazing, it's the lingering around to take in more, it's the imprint it leaves on you… forever.

Tony Miller
VP Digital Marketing & CRM, EMEA
Disney

For me, creativity is breaking rules constructively to create value. My mother always told me that I needed to 'take no for an answer' but I soon realised that interesting things happened when I ignored her advice! Early in my career I found myself attracted to questioning established norms. Challenging the status quo needs three supporting acts: courage to experiment, to fail and to sell your ideas; curiosity, which helps to make surprising connections; and serendipity – as much as we post-rationalise our successes in awards papers, if we're honest, sometimes a big dose of luck is involved.

The idea for MyWaitrose came from my past experience and a lucky catalyst – a headline for a white paper called 'Pointless Loyalty' caught my eye and made me think about how to apply the airline model to supermarkets. The experience-based grocery reward scheme was born. Without our supportive and entrepreneurial MD, Mark Price, and a team who had the courage to launch with the back-end IT held together with sticky tape, the idea might have fizzled. The final ingredient has to be fun: Einstein said, 'Creativity is intelligence having fun' – having the freedom to play with ideas and try new things is surely when we're all at our best.

Sarah Fuller
Group Brand Director
Aviva

Creativity is hard work, but it's what inspires and excites me the most in my role. Finding new ways to solve old problems, making linkages that haven't yet been made and creating something better as a result drives progress, and where would we be without that!

Paul Alexander
Director, Marketing Communications
Barclaycard

Syl Saller
Chief Marketing & Innovation Officer
Diageo

Creativity is something we all need, and very few of us think we have. But that is simply not true. It is down to us to find within, our own kind of creativity and nurture it. From a very young age, my brother, an illustrator, had magic in his hands that I didn't. I found my way in taking up pottery, with an eye for form that I developed over time.

Today, in the marketing world, I am in awe of our creative partners who dream ideas beyond my imagination and who make magic beyond my vision. I try not to get in their way. But still, I am aware I need to nurture my creativity and that of those around me to do the best work of their lives. It's looking for that special something in each individual – whether it's creativity in problem solving, in having a vision of the future, or in connecting the dots in ways that surprise and inspire. Creativity is within all of us and there is nothing more satisfying than creating an environment in which it can flourish.

Creativity is about seeing things differently, letting the imagination make connections that change the way we understand things and yet seem intuitive. And so, it brings art to the science of marketing. It is the magic that elevates us and brings energy to what we do every day.

Alex Naylor
Marketing Director
Barclaycard

Cheryl Calverley
CMO
Eve Sleep

Creativity is an excuse to escape. A chance to indulge your sense of 'other'. To do the thing you should never do in business. To be irrational, to wander, to head down blind alleys. To stop, to stare, to think. To breathe. Somewhere down one of these dark recesses, somewhere deep in a thought, or a line, or an image, you'll find a thread that connects, across space and time from one thing to another. And in that connection, in that excuse to open Pandora's box, you find the leaps that move life forward.

The horrifying thought however, is that we live all day being rational, calculating, analysing and don't realise. We don't realise that we're calculating and analysing the emotional reactions of others to creativity. To thoughts, ideas, stories. But, in this way, creativity flows through society, through the economy and out, into the 1s and 0s of a spreadsheet, and the pounds and pence of a balance sheet. Like alchemists, our job is to add creativity to the equation, and see the chemical reaction produce culture, value, worth, equity. We must continue to wield the creative sword as our weapon, confident that brute strength cannot overcome its finely crafted blade.

Creativity is creating white space ideas that move people emotionally.

John Rudaizky
Partner, Global Brand & Marketing Leader
EY

No one has the exclusive on creativity. It can come from any corner of the business. Wherever there is curiosity and a thirst for doing things better. Wherever taking risks is applauded and people push their ideas.

Our job as leaders is to create this environment, to cultivate this mindset and to champion the best ideas through to execution, whether that be a new product, a new campaign or a new service enhancement. Creativity gives businesses the edge, the spark and the momentum to outperform.

One of the joys of what I do is to be able to travel around the world, meeting fascinating people, from different cultures, ethnicities and beliefs with wonderfully different cuisines and languages, all in many ways dealing creatively with similar challenges, but with a kaleidoscope of different ways to address them. It has been written that creativity is characterised by the ability to perceive the world in new ways, find hidden patterns, make connections between seemingly unrelated phenomena, and to generate solutions.

Travelling the world definitely enables you to perceive the world in different ways. China, once the follower in the adoption of many industries, is now redefining the way customers interact with industry, creating seamless, frictionless customer experiences in industries such as coffee retail. Once the global domain of Starbucks, China now has retailers like S.Engine and Luckin Coffee, elevating the experience and eliminating queuing.

Another passion of mine, and the business I represent, Topgolf, is to connect people in meaningful ways, and some of the most rewardingly creative moments in my career have been making these connections between seemingly unrelated phenomena: such as introducing the beauty world to the world of toilet tissue; bringing the delights of The White Company products from our homes to the sky with BA; and, in the charity world, bringing Teenage Cancer Trust (TCT), Andrex and McFly together in an advert that raised both significant funds and profile for TCT.

Creativity is like pure oxygen, it breathes life into all of us.

Troy Warfield
President
TopGolf International

Ellie Norman
Director of Marketing & Communications
F1

Creativity, for me, is the ability to see things in a way that others cannot. It's an incredibly powerful and valuable skill that helps find new perspectives to create new possibilities and solutions to different problems. Creativity connects things together in order to derive new meaning or value. It's a phenomenon, a spark of an idea that you need to achieve your goals. Never easy, often bloody hard, however when nailed, it connects with people on different levels and leaves an impact.

Creativity is intangible. You can't touch it, but you can sure as hell feel it. It's the process that permits emotion and intent to collide with the realities of the physical world, and increasingly the digital world, to create an experience that drives a defined outcome.

It doesn't matter if it's visual, literary, aural or in any other medium; creativity under control results in an interaction that leaves you somewhere other than where you started – and at its best, it leaves you exactly where the artist intended.

Defining the outcome matters. It's through that process that you inextricably link the process of creativity with the output – which, unsurprisingly, we frequently shorthand as 'creative'. Creativity needs intent. Creativity to me is the purposeful combination of science, theory, process, inspiration, unintentional plagiarism, artistic flair, insight and originality, repeated and revised over and over again. And if you do all that without showing how, you're probably pretty good at it.

Ciaran Nelson
Director of Brand & Communications
Anglian Water

Andrea Newman
Global Head of Brand
HSBC

When I was born, my mother took me to see an astrologer. I still have the typescript from that meeting; I won't say how many years ago. The most pertinent thing the astrologer said was 'your daughter feels very strongly about only surrounding herself with beautiful things'.

It seems asinine to say creativity equates to beauty, but as I've thought about this; every time I reflect on 'what is creativity?' it's typically equated to things I found aesthetically desirable or invoked a positive or sensitive emotion. Beautiful objects, or words, or pictures that stay with you long after you have interacted with them.

I do think it's becoming an overused word though; especially in business. I prefer creativity when it is in its more purest form not when it is being applied to corporate speak or leadership lessons; then it's contrived. Creativity comes from insight into how humans react and manifests itself into beauty and clever thinking – that's how I see it.

The future belongs to the DJ's. Too often in business, really talented young people fail to do great creative work for fear of what others think. This fear is usually the unintended consequence of someone sharing an exciting idea but being 'taken down' by someone who should know better. They probably don't mean any harm, but a badly timed sarcastic comment from an experienced professional, can lead to a reluctance to share 'new' ideas in the future. You know what I'm talking about. 'We've all seen that before' or '__ did that at Cannes __ years ago'.

The problem is that most new creative ideas are hardly ever new anyway. Everybody steals from somebody else. Good artists copy, great artists steal, right? Whether you're an experienced creative director or a UX developer fresh from uni, we all create new things by reimagining existing ideas that we copy and transform into something different.

What is originality anyway? Undetected plagiarism. So, my wish is that we encourage more people to be curators not creators. We should celebrate the act of creating new media from old media, by curating content we love and remixing it into something new. Just like a DJ.

Jeremy Waite
Chief Customer Officer
IBM iX

Abi Comber
CMO
Oyster Yachts

Creativity is life.

What are we without it?

Just problems with no solutions, statements of facts with no meaning or expression.

It's empowering, it builds, it has energy and without it, life would be dull and rather monotone.

Margaret Jobling
CMO
Centrica Group

Real creativity is a gift, it is about creating a strong emotional connection with people, bringing to life the world in new and insightful ways. Easy to say but hard to do.

Creativity is imagination with a purpose. I believe we're all born with the innate ability to be creative – but nurturing that potential is vital for it to thrive. Imagination opens our minds to a wealth of innovative ideas and opportunities. But imagination needs to be encouraged and celebrated, particularly in childhood, and not only in those showing a talent with words, or crayons, or within the confines of the classroom.

Creativity brings joy to our personal lives, allowing us to express ourselves and explore new possibilities. However, it is equally central to business success. In an uncertain work environment (and who knows what skills will be needed in future?) creativity remains essential because we'll always need to explore new ideas, inspire passion and break new ground to solve problems.

Our industry is all about engaging people emotionally, grabbing their attention and changing their behaviour. Technology and data are exciting as enablers to marketing success, yet are ineffective without brilliant creativity that makes you gasp, cry, smile and, ultimately, engage.

Hilary Cross
Global Marketing Director
British Council

Toby Horry
CMO
TU

Creativity has two quite separate meanings which often get conflated. On one hand, there are creators whose talent is to make things that didn't previously exist.

On the other, there are creative thinkers who tend not to bring new things to the world but are good at solving problems in innovative ways. I've always been more of the latter and wish I could be more of the former. But increasingly modern organisations need both.

As marketers, it's easy to say how much we love great creativity. It's another thing entirely to be part of creating it. It means standing up, fighting, going the extra mile and, ultimately, being willing to stake your reputation on new spaces, new frontiers. This is the difference between mediocre and great marketers.

In my experience, it comes down to one thing: the nurturing of creative genius; encouraging it, not being afraid of it; demanding it, not diluting it. In my book, there is no great creativity that doesn't stem from a touch of creative genius, so inspired and unexpected that it forces us to look at what we thought we knew from a new and surprising perspective. Clever gets you part of the way. Clever is easier to buy. True creative genius takes you somewhere electrifying. And that's sometimes scary.

Our world is becoming one of tech and data, which prioritise and revere the knowns, leaving little room for creative genius. In fact, as numbers acquired the cool factor, they have pushed creativity into the shade. They are not natural bedfellows. Therefore, it is our challenge to manage the relationship between the two worlds. If we don't – in an industry ever more in pursuit of mathematical certainty – the very joy of advertising is at risk, for both marketers and the consumer. Defending that joy relies on all of us guarding creative genius. And protecting creative genius is – for me – the most rewarding part of our job.

Jayne O'Keeffe
Marketing Director
Mothercare

For me, creativity is about expression. True and differentiated expression of an idea. Creativity is the expression of an idea in a unique and original way. Truly great creative can often be spontaneous and it's important that great creativity is given a chance to shine and thrive. I recently learnt this first hand, when I started to learn how to do improvised comedy. In improvised comedy, your creativity comes from a single word or idea that 2–3 people need to bring to life with techniques like 'yes and' helping to build on and not quash others people's creativity, meaning the full creative idea is expressed completely. Inspiring stuff.

Great creativity is an idea so unique it can positively shift perceptions, moving people into action. When I worked in insurance, great creativity took a brief as simple as 'create a water cooler moment' and gave me a Morgan Freeman impersonator dubbed More Th>n Freeman. It's what's given us over 6 years of strong brand health too, at TSB by breaking the conventional norms in bank advertising. Something that's vital to achieve in a category where people are more likely to leave their husband or wife than leave their bank.

Pete Markey
CMO
TSB

Creativity is an unfettered imagination combined with the confidence to push boundaries. It's what children have in spades and why we should listen to them more.

Alison Lomax
Director, Lifestyle Retail
Google

Ian Armstrong
Former Global Head of Advertising
Jaguar Land Rover

To me, creativity is making something out of nothing. If you ask an adult what they can make from a paper clip many would struggle, if you ask a child you will get 100s of ideas in minutes. Where would humankind be without the space to think, imagine and try?

Fiona Spooner
Global Marketing Director, B2C
Financial Times

For me, creativity is about pulling together previous experiences – the way we recognise ideas and the influences of others and fuse them together to make something new. It's very rare that there's a new discovery overnight, it's usually a fusion of ideas and experiences that have come before – creativity is needed to spot which of those ideas and experiences will work best together. But creativity can't live on its own.

A contextual understanding of the market, or audience, or product is key for creativity to work, or it'll be brushed off as 'weird thinking'. This usually means looking at the world from a different perspective than that of your customers or your team. Take that view to come up with a new approach, or way of thinking.

We traditionally think of creativity in context of the arts, but we see creativity all around us, for example, being creative in the way you analyse your data can give you a competitive advantage. Our best creative work comes from teams, when we come together and use our diverse backgrounds and blend ideas into something new. I love it when that happens.

Creativity is that unexpected thought, turn of phrase, piece of art/music/fashion/protest that makes us sit up straighter. It can deepen our passion for something or someone; or throw open the door to an entirely new one.

It inspires equal amounts awe and envy. And when it's at its best, like the B-side of Abbey Road, it's endlessly enjoyable.

Michelle McEttrick
Group Brand Director
Tesco

Gary Nall
Head of Western Europe
GVC

Creativity in marketing has to come with positive results. In some boardrooms, you start talking about creativity and eyes will roll. Winning hearts and minds is important.

There is no better way than demonstrating the power of marketing than with results aligned to creative excellence. In my day-to-day, I love to see creativity at work when it comes to problem solving.

To me, creativity is the power to imagine the unimaginable, and the power to see what can be beyond what has ever been.

In a world that's focussed on facts and data, creativity is the bit of magic that connects the dots and turns what everyone knows into new possibilities that no one could see.

Claudia Struzzo
Group Brand & Engagement Director
Kingfisher plc

Ian McGregor
CMO
Green Man Gaming

Creativity for me is like oxygen, a building block, it creates self-esteem and confidence for the individual, cohesion for the community and value to the economy, which helps us all live to our fullest potential.

Creativity to me is building emotional connections with customers that leaves a positive and lasting imprint.

Creativity moves people, creates feelings and makes memories.

Amanda Jennings
Director of Marketing Communications
The Co-operative Group

Jamie Taylor
Retail, Property & Wholesale Director
L'Occitane

Working in London, Paris and Geneva, I'm privileged to move amongst some of the world's most exciting creative people and ideas. Dazzling imaginations, innovative artwork, dangerous new directions. Some of it is 'art for arts sake', and I love it. But the creativity I'm always most interested in is creativity that sells. With high street retail under ever-growing threat from the online challenge, this has never been a more important distinction to make. Yes, you can get attention if you shout loud enough. Yes, you can win all those shiny awards. But that's not enough. Unless your creativity is relentlessly promoting brand identity and awareness, consumer preference, competitive differentiation, and so on – all of which ultimately deliver sales and profits – it's not serving your business.

To put it another way: creative is as creative does. So my advice is, interrogate every creative proposal, even the ones that knock your socks off. Especially those ones. Are they really in tune with your audience? Do they speak their language? Above all, does that stunningly original concept sustain its compelling force right through to the cash register? If you don't get the right answers, think again. Because that's the great thing about creativity: there's always another fresh new idea waiting to surprise you.

Celine Dallas
Head of Brand
Tesco

Creativity was narrowly defined in my school day, and I'm only in my 40s! Kids have a better understanding of its power and breadth today. My sister, an amazing artist, was acknowledged as a creative sort. I was able to develop my leadership skills, which required problem solving skills, but I could not draw or paint.

The 'creative label' never seemed to apply to me. Yet I read voraciously and was drawn to words and ideas. I decided to study marketing and psychology, and have not looked back. Marketers mix the commercial drive of business with a curiosity about people, and what motivates them. They harness this insight to fuel brand and product (or service) ideas. A sensitivity to aesthetics and the role of visual language helps too.

I love what I do! I hope that my kids find their way to work that intrigues them, keeps them asking questions and working creatively to solve problems.

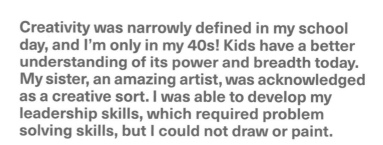

Zaid Al-Qassab
CMO
BT

For me, creativity is what happens when you encourage someone to express themselves, to develop ideas and executions in which they find inspiration, delight or simply amusement. There's such diversity within human beings that if you create the conditions for freedom of expression, you can't help coming up with things that cause a meaningful reaction in others. That response can be anything from desire to repulsion, and all shades in between.

Of course, in a business context, you might have a particular objective in mind, usually engagement of some kind, or an impulse to find out more, or maybe a sense of belonging. But there's no doubt in my mind that the way to it is via encouraging self-expression. I've found that all the best creative work results from letting people just get on with it. That's how the magic happens.

Creativity catches in your throat, makes the hairs on your neck stand up, brings a tear to your eye and puts an extra beat in your heart.

Creativity is the story you can't forget, the inspiration you can't ignore.

Catherine Kehoe
Managing Director, Group Brands & Marketing
Lloyds Banking Group

For creativity to flourish, it needs the space to breathe and the permission to break boundaries. Only then can you produce work that is truly defining and which will stand the test of time.

To take these bold steps off the high board, you need to have a deep self-belief to see things through when all around might be caution and conservatism. And, for it to really find form and succeed, it requires unfailing commitment and tenacious execution.

Keith Kropman
Director Marketing & Human Resources
Vitality

Without creativity we create a sea of sameness, a world of boring brands that fail to capture people's imagination. Creativity can fundamentally change how we feel about something. As John Hegarty so eloquently said, 'What the heart feels today, the head will know tomorrow'.

Penny Herriman
Customer Director
White Stuff

For me, creativity is the lifeblood of marketing and one of the ingredients that makes our role in the organisation truly special.

Brilliant creative work is of course imaginative and inspiring, but I always look for three magic ingredients:

Distinctiveness. Getting noticed and standing out. In the context of brands, building fame consistently over time and creating valuable assets.

Bravery. Every time I have seen great creative work it has required bravery. Brave agencies who are not afraid to challenge, or think the unthinkable, and brave clients that can spot great work and are prepared to back themselves to go for it!

Determination. Ideas without application are just dreams. Delivering great creative work requires energy, determination and self-belief. It doesn't happen on its own and we call work 'work' for a reason!

Above all, though, creativity is fun and exciting. It inspires the organisations we work in and the customers we serve. It is a massive part of why we get up every day and do what we do.

Nathan Ansell
Marketing Director
Marks & Spencer

Creativity is the alchemy of taking our thoughts and ideas and turning them into something. For me it is an emotion, a process, an action and a way of seeing things that can help us tell our stories and ideas. It's the intersection of where our dreams meet reality. Creativity is the magic of life – it's my oxygen!

Nishma Robb
Marketing Director
Google

Creativity liberates us from the confines of everyday expectations; the ones that demand we think and behave in certain ways. In a world increasingly skewed by the pursuit of perfection and success, the model of replication stifles individuality. And with the relentless appetite for evidence, proof points, data, frameworks and boundaries, creativity provides the perfect antidote to self doubt, bias and prejudice. Giving us the confidence to be ourselves and combat the forces of conformity.

Creativity simply gives us the permission and freedom to think, feel and work differently, to discover our potential and the impact we can have on an otherwise unthinkably dull world.

Richard Taylor
Executive Director Fundraising,
Marketing & Communications
Macmillan

Credits

OYSTERCATCHERS

RANKIN

FIFTH

SEA

PureprintGroup

&Printed

G . F
SMITH
1885 ONWARDS

MACMILLAN
CANCER SUPPORT

ISBN: 978-0-9955741-4-4

This idea started as a chat between Rankin and Suki about Suki's Mum and has ended up as a exhibition and book with some of the leading players from the marketing industry.

Oystercatchers and Xeim would like to thank:

The awesome Rankin for working his magic; and all his amazing team including Nicola, Beth, Christine, Ellen and Jordan for all their support.

Suki for using her black book to encourage and corral the great and good of the marketing industry to take part and to all the CMO's who took the time to attend the shoot and write about their creative beliefs.

Nick and Marco Antonio, the amazing glam team, for making everyone feel relaxed and looking gorgeous.

The Fifth who have been our brilliant partner in this book.

SEA for designing this beautiful book.

Pureprint for their exceptional print quality. &Printed for their production support, and GF Smith for kindly supplying the paper.

Hogarth for supporting the exhibition at FOM and the Oystercatchers Awards.

Lizzie Debonnaire for chasing up all the quotes.

A special mention to Phil, Becca, and the rest of the Oystercatchers team for making both the exhibition and book a reality.

Thanks to Jaz, Sam and Feilim who have supported Suki throughout.

We believe that creativity is a force for good – it touches our very soul. And so, we're proud to say that this glorious Rankin initiative has helped raise money for Macmillan Cancer Support – a charity close to our hearts.

Here's to creativity!!!

Love,
Suki and Rankin

Some of the CMO's have changed roles since these portraits were taken. All efforts have been made to make sure information is up to date at time of printing.